Weather's Feather

poems by Mitch Corber

Other books by Fly By Night Press

Something Eve Packer
Groove, Bang and Jive Around (e-book) Steve Cannon
Divine Comedy Ron Kolm
One-Bedroom Solo Sheila Maldonado
Impious Pilgrim George Spencer
Black Ice Barbara Purcell
Waterworn Star Black
Broken Noses and Metempsychoses Michael Carter

Other books by Mitch Corber

br cl (1977)

10-Minute Discourse (1979)
(Broadside)

Rude (1982)
(Book of poems, prose, b&w photo-graphics
and concrete poetry)

Knit-Wit (1984)

Concrete Musings (1985-86)
(Suite of poetic street posters wheatpasted
onto Village tenement walls)

Quinine (2009)
(Thin Air Media chapbook)

Many thanks to the editors of the journals in which
some of these poems first appeared: *Vanitas, Polarity,
Blackbox Manifold, E-ratio, First Literary Review-East,
ditch, Listenlight, BlazeVOX, faroutfurtheroutoutofsight,
Mirage, Brownstone Anthology, White Rabbit, gobbet*
and *Columbia Poetry Review.*

Minnie —
You warm the cockles
of my shy heartstrings.
Your smile is a gift and
a blessing to me. You help
me keep my head on straight,
and see the light between
us before I have a chance
to open my eyes.

Weather's Feather

poems by Mitch Corbett

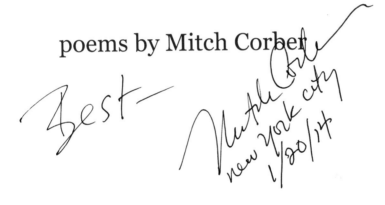

Best —

Mitch Corbett
new york city
1/30/14

Fly By Night Press

ISBN: 978-0-9637405-4-0

First Edition

Acknowledgments

The author would like to thank the following people for
for their timely suggestions on the manuscript. My gratitude
goes to my readers, the poet-editors Cindy Hochman,
Karen Neuberg, George Spencer and Ron Kolm; and especially
to George and Ron for helping me through the printing
process. A big thanks goes to Steve Cannon of Fly By Night
Press, the faithful publisher who believes in me. Bravo
to designer Mark Bloch for his aesthetic fortitude.
And my deep appreciation goes to Minnie Berman for her
valuable feedback all through this endeavor.

Cover art by Mark Bloch
and Mitch Corber

www.tribes.org

Fly By Night Press
(a subsidiary of A Gathering of the Tribes)
P.O. Box 20693
Tompkins Sq. Station
New York, NY 10009

(Continued from back cover)

Weather's Feather is Mitch Corber's playful testimonial to "riding the wakened blend of backbreak," ringing the doorbell and the dinner bell and the churchy bells that summon you to testify to whichever Muse has chosen you. The poet pays fluid lip service to many and various influential channel spanners, from "drip-dry druids" to "bees in bobbing trees" as he wanders, wondering what became of wonder in these shriveled times.

These carefully calibrated poems — whose subtle rhythms and internal rhymes occasionally seem to duplicate the sonic effect of a steel bar wrapped in velvet being run along a picket fence — contain a pulsing element of joy that surfaces intermittently, in susurrations that suggest a quiet but sensual exuberance ready to punch a railroad through the text itself.

—Max Blagg

Mitch Corber comes to us from out of nowhere, yet very much from out of somewhere. He can write love "in the proxy of praxis"— where lovemaking is akin to poesis. A sensitive ear to assonance and rhyme, and love of the weird word, fuels Corber's lyric metric. He does not so much explore as navigate. He seems to dwell in the metaphysic, rather than the street, though his sense of human, and particularly romantic, relation is vivid. His metaphysic is a valuable tool for living, existing as it must in what he terms "the lethal diamond dream."

—Vincent Katz

Mitch Corber, grassroots documentarian of East Village poetry scene for decades, here shows that his vérité eye goes bongo gonzo when flipped into his interior abyss. He asks, "Have you seen my pesky porcupine,/her spiny tingle, those naughty needles?" and while everybody else might just say Noooo, for Mitch it's an everyday experience. What's in those needles? Surrealist syringes, jazz bops and verbal nonstops...!

Teddy B (Berrigan) puts in an appearance (on Avenue C) — he is *La Bohème*, with Corber strutting like Lord Buckley to get hiperama. His are the Beatles of "The Eggman." Take two poems and call him in the morning. Name a poem "Pyrex Bowl." Don't take an answer for an answer. *Goo-goo-ga-joob*. Mitch Corber is the Mad Taxidermist, and language is his prey.

—Bob Holman

Corber was introduced to poetry through nursery rhymes. He took off from there and never looked back. His flights of fancy display love, loneliness, impermanence, the joys of imagination, and unexpected ascents and descents. No one ever knows where one of his poems will land. And no two trips are alike. This is a book for worldly travelers who never tighten their seatbelts.

—George Spencer

Contents

CHAPTER 1: *Whims of Intimacy*

CHAPTER 2: *Journey to the Id*

CHAPTER 3: *Highwire Acts*

for Minnie

1

Whims of Intimacy

Yawning Songbirds

Veiled moon over Vaporous Valley
A myth of impeccable depth
Hasty cookies cornstarch
alarming inventories of sordid crave

Imagine the explosive hose
a yawning lawn
of early dawning songbirds
looking for a clearing

Indoors I shun a one-way weekend binge
for the twinge of meditation
Creaky cabinets of *look and ye shall*
plainly chase an acquired taste

Catching cod in a leaky canoe
tossing odd tributes to liquid Neptune
Easy lifeboat throat
of sporadic nibbling

Curvatures, reticular
in their particular pose
throw a rosy glow
on social mores

Geiger counter passes over
the patient's prone body
Cobalt sky
possesses culpability

I hustle a Monday summit
up a seasonable mountainside
tipping my hand to the landfill
scorched by an ill-timed torch

Harvest

I lace words   these poems
are a harvest of happenstance
a mowing of muses

With each sequester
I invest a brash attack
These seeds will flower

Porcupine

Have you seen my pesky porcupine,
her spiny tingle, those naughty needles?

The hoofbeat of heathen freshets
in depthing ratchets?

The quasi-spontaneous
neo-periphery of liaisons?

Antic waif of feudal make
    I budge a cruder order.
        The less I laugh, a craft I ply.

A fiery crown of frowning tones
along the muscled edge of drudge.

The Wonder Fear

Tumble down the Wonder Fear, barely
borrowed from your commerce eyes,
a pause in my century stare, a schism vision
of a puffball plantation, wary of
the tic-tac laptop consequences.

Discern the mere holler of a dollar down,
soundless pestilence in the palm court.
Eerie trajectories of a cramped corridor,
the surge inflicted by inflections past.
In person, on point.

I'm here wherever weaving trends send
a message to my moron toes, the news frozen.
Closures surround the common corners
voicing the swoop of an anthem
— damn the manageable meanings.

Could the very workaday perk up
my errant ears? Can the stance of a dancer
manipulate the center stage?
Or must I mop the millionaire's forehead,
unmask his subcutaneous pores?

I'd drink a sinkful of gladdened magnets,
darkly draw the curtains for emerging moonbeams
scheming to envelop the pulp and panache,
in future volumes well-versed
in the doggerel of a fogbound clown.

Waive the price of long-grain rice,
the burrow widened by a wiseguy mole,
then heed the bellow of celery stalks their
talkative lipgloss. Heap wishes on a silver star
alluring skies, the nascent night.

Pretend words are woolly stems in the bin
of buy and sell, clever puns impending pearls
of woodshed wisdom, morphed into
border cops in shiny badge arrangements
— true to the nicotine peril.

Wriggle the pencil point forward with the hiss
of hands swiping the likely plight
of credit cards enlightened by sight gags
ingenious in their common denominator
of trip stumble and fall.

Lips clash of wishes tossed like ripe squash
in sautéed skillets, the perk a pile
of wiccan knives in size 8 sheaths,
itching to inscribe their drifty slogans
into an arm of justice.

Risky Roses

This quick of fidelity
catches me in naked roar
a-pouring of pursuing
The lid unlatched
A passion nesting to be taken
or risky roses in tow

Strew these weeds
they're fakers
in the harvest
    of alarming
           yes

It's Levitation

It's levitation, larynx of lush archery
Yellowed perch, parrot tipsy
    Locally
    a blinkin' eye

Would dawns announce a cowbell? A low choir
of dewy eye & salty hymn on the wane?
    Theories fly haphazard
    in Kansas disasters

Yes need teeters in a twig, resister to a thick
windy grip on its membrane nervings
    Connective urgings angling rivers
    purge where they surge

But grace is not too great for Grandma
Her cure for tired feet, a flash of ancient action
    Before the weathered pages
    of re-telling

Our guest is October's gust, a tug at the cuff
Late cocktails accrue a rash of ashes
    A speech of worn knuckles,
    curiosity, creeds

Stock footage of hats, rows of empty seats
The bristle of a Fall sale, a whale of a deal
    Bear a brand name, Betty
    Buy! Buy! Buy!

Flustered

Trip-switch. Diptych. Noose with a persistent pulse
and a knot to trot. If flustered. Twice blistered.
Medical leave and a cheetah's itch for rich reward.
Concatenation. Articulation. A crumb and a numb
finger's figure-it-out. About-face and a fear resting
easy. The teary permissions-proud portrait of
an ornery tortoise. A thwart in the throat, remote.
"Abort," said the legal beagle.

Butterfly

for my mother, Anne

Wind can utter a butterfly
The soluble air
Apparent in the thing of wings
Its nest a breast of flowers
Or heave of ferns
The breathing singing the stems make
The flutter stutters the savoir-faire.

Airborne, the storm resides in sighs
Silver clouds caress the western sky
As lime trees mind the seasons
Everything grows with a little pain
The rain barrels filling tipping flowing
A drop becomes a drip, a drink becomes a cup
The camper sure of early snow.

We row our burly boats
At the fevered pitch of risk
The panther capering at the shore
Preying eyes above, the eagle glued
To all-ensuing rumors and romance
When swoops the leaper of cocoons
Our flighty friend, the bender in the wind
The bringer of the Spring.

Hologram Hangover

Rifts drift a pinned
and versatile ladder murk
in the park dark as the passion
of new neighbors

Dimmed of a sinful bagel
a pearl of a whirlwind
unfurls in the lurid latchkey
loss of a tossed hope

Tons of lovestung hucklebuck
a bones-free wheedling
in terms of clandestine
mentions of a clothesline

Dry eyes in a durable
worldly wallop the fame game
inferring tendrils of lamentable
pencil-thin arrangements

Lurking flammable circuits
in a drench of testy
nettings in a skinflint saga
of elasticity

The remnant shapes
of wayfaring words
the mere shadow
of a hologram hangover

Shifting Pretty

Ifs ifs ifs are an index
of insecurity. Commas
shifting pretty in
a linseed bagatelle.

God I'm emasculated
dead to the tinny tongue
of inconsequence.

I'm assured of
a nervous never-say-die,
a Prilosec of impotence,
a pinebox of
inappropriate puns.
A lung-scraping
puncture smitten
of a lingering chill.

Dizzy after-spell
shellac a-sniffin'
tintinnabulation erect
or speculative in this
rocky colostomy.

Tarnish and tamper
bright as the landfill
lisping a gutteral rush.
Enough is a narc
certifying his own
sleight-of-hand burden.

Love's Late Rain

loser, did you earn
    the creepy drizzle
        of love's late rain?

anger fondles the knife
    in a trinket
        of tiny suggestion

will her heels click
    inconstant to his
        burnt arrangements?

shhhh: neighbors
    asleep in their
        meek evasions

have you heard the dead wood
    of no one drumming? no time
        ticking? no stone turning?

systems leave me
    silent to the nuance
        of a person

they're absolutely two separate people
    pawning their switchblade hearts
        for some heat

love's bottom
    is a talkative
        autumn

her plum is your
    patience, a strumming
        undulation

sparrow, would you
    land on a man's
        sweaty hand?

if not
    wand, then
        weapon

her circus wisdom
    over every
        prism

deftly unweaponing
    his fright, unlearning
        the certain systems

her hearing is impaired
    by his warm collection
        of nearings

is this
    the spill of heaven's
        will?

Itch

The wholly pitch of cell-to-cell
yields life's very affirmation
Emits a stitch, a mosaic of moods
within the itch of the instant

A Hundred Tongues

A hundred tongues lead me to steer
the impossible far-gone conclusions of a sleuth
chewing on a clue. In turning an inner ear
to the serious nature of plates
I break one, to see what it's made of.

A fluffy pink arousal is a cotton-candy dancer.
A mordant everlasting is a faster buck untendered.
Zones moan a stasis, *rot-got-yer-tongue,*
tumultuous minutes of a popular clock sold
in most Ma & Pa hardware operations.

The feeble and the senile in a circle.
A terrible sucking attenuation.
I've watched my insomnia breed a block
of theaters, wished my restless fiber
to wrestle with the gods.

So I've softened expectations lately,
a scale hovering on a number. Fumbling,
I've fastened "laughed at" to my magic strap.
A hinge of shyest flavors infiltrates
the zoo of higher learning.

Heavens erupt to the sumptuous past.
Museums are leaning to historicize.
Slinky tiger cat-licks his claws
hogging all the best kill.
Teeth seem straighter when they smile.

Mercury Moth

Even licky-tip licorice suspends the pensive enemy.
A balm sooner than a bite. Fashionista. Sausage pizza.
Road narrows as you while away mileage. A mercury
moth in a 60-watt outage. Thursday jurist, no alarmist.
Self-made servant, he earnestly prevails. A phantom
slant on Atlanta packrats. Peach blossom. Perky autumn.
Men with an entirely gaudy glare.

Eclipse

Eclipse ... damage ... lens ...
you start ... move ...

"I got it all on tape"

Your removals are a habit
now

The early mystics all agree
that the sun is steadily
damaging our eyes

         ... and for no
apparent reason the lights
just went xxxxx

I have the secret
information

How do we always narrowly miss
in the hallway?

It's like asking helmeted men
to think without
their helmets

Baby

That starving reaching
miscued for reconstruction

As they wryly situate
in their neighborings of civility.

But lately I find that baby wants
every valve occupied, especially
the salivation of slippery prayers.

A Safety of Signs

The word is rife in a safety of signs, a startle
of skies, a loose inner bug, a wild ill-advise.

The rising resentment, a cough in the cloth,
a wool of white Fridays at the wheel of redemption.
A link to food in the chump-chain.

In a rash of upheaval, the wearing away
of the dutiful crust, the mucous of cause in a mollusk
of moves.

A froth of draft, a fix of drift, the click of cash
and a drawer of goods. The looming crawl of a lowing
herd, the cowboy clash of a dusty dog.

Sigh palpable in a whiff of retrieval. Zen buddha
witless in a lapse of white lies.

These husks these rinds all carry the flurry of fury,
the lead in my pencil, the nerve to be heard.

A wicker of wonders, a stun of giraffe. The rusty
mare in a moo of glue. Which-end-is-up in a drown
of coffeecup.

A wearing away of the peachfuzz of promise,
the ominous frost, a layer of skin at the wit's end of lust.

A lampshade of dust in a follicle frenzy. Fabulous
craters to tease our reminders. The flotsam of jetty,
the frenzy of frogs.

I look to the rest just to test the remainder.

Gentle Me a Symmetry

Gentle me a symmetry of delayed
desire lit by a clientele of electricity
A waylaid case of first friction
glimpsed in dense and tender systems

Skein

A skein of mangy moments interrupts a tray
of fancy deli. Feldspar feels more like shale,
a shallow pan of foolers' gold. Never on Sunday.
Nunca domingo, señorita, no sign of relief.

Pardon me I've bred a tension
spanked with barking knives. Skin limits
a green counsel of invigorant sounds.
Simulcast elections rig the Figure 9.

Nil and not a factor
I'm prone to moan clueless in this clinch.
It's a cinch I gather at the bedpost
a curious grin of begging mouth.

Training for the main stage a million legs
shake off the shingles. I plead a deep & dancing icon
bubbling in its brew, or fooled, a mighty lightness
succumbing to the running commentary.

Please stomach the hardened violence,
the heaped bleatings, the severed nobility
concerning my salient body. Do limit your
furrowed-brow bullyings, *mon amour.*

Southward flees the frosted seasons
lost in slumber's chill.
Ill-timed, a tempestuous fist
resists the doubter's dilemma.

Clue

Four doors to the writhing right of center.
A painter by heart, a crier by trade.

Paid for and done, the hungry hundred
Waitin' t' be fed. Pinge of soft pine.

Ruse by rouge, the usual clues.
The nature of oranges & yes, the syringe.

Cannibals

Cannibals sit and chat while the mentality
of a rat skittles and trickles through
the trash. Seven dead in East Dallas.

      Hiatus of toast.

The collapse is unusual in that
ever since Seattle went to the sea,
my sinuses vacillate miserably!

      Aloof turf.

And blue is its double-edged womb.
Carved in starvation. "This craze
is a circus trance from a study
of Somali dance."

      Heavy breather.

When whipped. Save the chips
for. Factory cats.

      And you meant it.

Thrive

A braid of empty
thrive
upends the gristle

Lint elegantly suggests
loose plex and vexed
particulation

Worry of a Wart

As cause will stir the worry of a wart
dormant ants will soon scurry up a leery hill
braving the raised tabernacle of a scuttled sigh

The titter of hysteria
sprawls above spread-eagle advertisements
which dig at the wig and cradle hallelujah
in any ready guise

The landfill's solid with sifters
The less-tense troubadour trusting
in the dharma drink

Prismatic antics a chorus of texts
Limbs fly and dim the lie of dreams unfluttered
and gummed of reprieve

Should I die out of doors
lest a gesture a lesson of loosening down
and letting the fond flowers fish for a wish?

Pigeons in their hinges harken to a beat,
a jingo jewel, a collapsing criminal
element of temple resentments
en-neighbored of enamored heave and haw

Why pursue the repartee headstrong
in a homegrown gather of a Greek garden?

Mist and the mountains hiss accord of a doorway
Undone are the stunned and the staggering

Recoil

Sex takes an arrangement a positioning.
Nibbly teeny sheets tucked in tiny corners.
Lots of spunk, recoiling into the audiophile.
Alert closeted monks durable and so
true to the grit of wisdom much in the way
I wooed you hooted and howled dirty
pleasures.

Inner Ear

let us be society's cripples
the dimple over the rock its buzz
in the nuance of a rage in whirling thirsts

let us craze their straight fingers
with the pirouette of a nude
in the office

the weak whiskerings streaming
through the semaphore
the nurture of my truest rumors

I speak a special lurid logic
of damnations, dizzy angers,
the sweep of prayers upon the inner ear

would I cross an eagle with a whim,
the sinister wrist, the uneven
chin, the motive in spin?

Burdened Peace

A claim of famined wind
besets the ways of draped
remorse. Close-cast
the broom retools the dusty.

A pillared blizzard rips
the engines off a sonic mast.
The breast of rude esteem
now breathes a stubborn ringing.

Terror grips the open palm.
Twilight tips the ledge
of thrust. A burdened peace
snaps a bandaged casing.

First Face Forward

I am your cribbed
and burrowed ribcage
cuddling a phrase as a flying cry for light
Of biting half my teeth are tingling
in this singing soul

You lift the latch of hunted aspirations
shunted by me yearly
I'm deceived on the surface
by a shifting whim
occupying heady ground

I seem the friendly ghost
of a toasted intolerant glitch
Yet my smile recognizes
how wry and airy
is the temporary

I'm turning to a blot of skippy phrasing
a bonus entertainment
to contain an autumn in your
springing step

You, my dusky iris
embracing gains of god-search
in an ultimate ether

Apologies for the free-flowing joy
seems to jab at my hearty resilience
in a crushing gulp
Inhaling not the all of you
but insisting for time's sake
to travel it slo-mo

To skip past the gut check
of the reigning wrecking ball
in beggy plea
        to ease us our places
        to unhasten desire
        as we whiten the fire

Too haunted by *I could've been's...*
so harried I blab the gladhand grinning
No sin to put my first face forward
in awe of what can be

Yet can't the bees in bobbing trees
intercede a softened
rock candy landing
in the *become of wonder?*

2

Journey to the Id

Delayed Desires

A slip-stride in the light tickle
sleeping in a sly itch.
A friction distanced by its very destination.
Flurried robes a fuzz of heard hush
lending an eon-ear to the rigors
of alternate approval.

Knees jimmy at the mince of panic
a pain-free upheaval
the swirl of a rapid du jour
a frantic posting in the pockets of perspiration.

Girls — their come-with-it module
cloth de rigueur — of a softer voice
in the calamitous crunch,
a puncture-wound
retraced in an estrogen minute.

I'm an imminent menu of delayed desires,
a jiggy manifestation of a homely space
between the teeth, a frame of hayseeds
splashing stray soliloquys
at nervy passengers, testy
and of a mild terminal nature.

She shrugs a hazard-guess:
Wrestle me to the floor
more midget than man-eater,
a soothing nuance, a seething prayer.

Capacity Soot

Fumes rim the running heel of sprouting
silicon, suffering rejection in the form
of boredom continental

Mental mushrooms swim dumbfounded
in soundless sleep as the limber chimneysweep
paupers his weary way to capacity soot

arson is a lesson learned

arson is a lesson learned
in tourniquet worship, loaves
of sodabread bobbing atop
the kerosene waters

prim and prune of noonday
fires fingers licking
red and yellow bunting,
flames uttering the fluttering

drifts neanderthal sleds
and snowbirds wordy infinitude
semi-linear proto-conscious
dirigibles of quasi-jive

dark permissions shout
of famine breezes
fanning fury to new heights
and chatty magpies

Sensing Fumes

You're the wanted I'm
the haunted half-breed needy
wet behind the nearsighed novice
province of a pea-feeling princess
embedded on an eiderdown

I'm cabbage to your courage,
my silent leaf is low and lonely rows
of silk catch the light in gallant
glimpses here's my handy bandaid
sensing fumes in rumor's carriage

I'm a jailbird witness dog-eared
pages landing hard and harder
feelings speaking to my quiet life
within the limbs and spinning now
I'm seeking knowledge of your lips
pried open, just the latch undone

There's Teddy B on Avenue C

poet Ted Berrigan 1934-1983, a portrait

Before computers brought the fingers
an easy mastery of the keys
New York underground was 'zines-a-poppin', man
    a direct connect...hunt-n-peck

    In limbs lie whims of muscle motion

Ol' Ted Berrigan, he'd whistle in the thistle,
a steamy jugular of roaring arpeggios
    Visionary poet slippin' freely along Avenue C
    among the neo-Beat literati.

Sideburns spun from ginger candy
Juggling odd jobs, talkin' non-stop...
Teddy B hummed hybrid in his heyday
swiggin' words like brandy

    Time to launch my tough-as-nails torpedo.

With a verby vibe
    it was a matter of chatter
In one great manic moment
Teddy B seized the day
with his brave new American Sonnet....
    he meant no malice...just ask Alice

La Bohème was his name....

    A prevalent crayon of scrambled time.

    ...beyond the poem chase,
        he knew no other line of
            workaday prophetics.

Towels of a Drying

She unseats me neatly
from my surface resistance
Hinged twinge of havoc

Eager diminish
stiff wish

Towels of a drying
unsoil the pores

Lathers spell parlez-vous
in a rinse

Gender moan
Hormone

Moon a
honeywheat muffin

Weather's Feather

for Dylan Thomas

Chase change in chiméra's conduit,
peak at the pluck of weather's feather.
Swap opportunities in dizzy song,
a surrogate leaping deeper-than-thought,
conscious as a wheel cog,
consummate as a cheering union.

Ride the wakened blend of backbreak,
for godsakes a siren shimmering on the wane.
The brain drain abandoned to a tortoise shell
of hellbent Wednesdays, a spooning outcrop
of the thrumming dumbing down
of bound sweat and braggage.

Move me as any movie
from a voyeuristic crouch
in trial-bubble bingo,
the ringtone nesting in a pensive
lemondrop opportunity.

While the peal of an early bell
deciphers its piety in a pricked blister,
to etch a wretch his bloody bond of crotch and hairs,
assembling in a wintry blink
this bare reference to the shin of shy resurfacings,
the bleating treatment of a bully goat.

Slashed as an asking price, tonight's itinerary
spites the sticker shock of drip-dry druids
in fluid robe, giving Death the breath it dreads,
in a seismic nocturnal foraging,
maintaining a moth-eaten mortgage
of the sordid spackled facts.

Act One

He nuzzles, she puzzles.
He's marking, she's barking.
They'll hug, rub and build,
or perhaps merely drag a bugged
sleep in the creaking.

They've found a cure for porridge:
Courage.

Toenails and Teeth

What she touches rushes up
my spleen as spinal rivets
resist the twist
of a hundred screws

Individual shy and of a primal
point these etiquettes
all eschew the warp of ordinary love,
its cupcakes, its easy oaths

He's casual as a claw
in the raw testimony of rigid thumbs
spinning her jewels
in secondary school

We've rubbed into a doubleplay
the sync of lips grappling with a risky
plum, the reward of which
is the sum of forgiveness

When friend will you write
with your teeth
and your toenails
in the proxy of praxis?

No shoe followed shoe in the roundly
ragged routine of seeming to spin
intoxicating, as if the front were
buttoned at the back

Lissom

She nettles at the fitful ridge
the sputter of a hooligan hunt,
the fumbling only totalling a nifty
fifty of uppity mischief wrenched
to the nth of enemy fire.

Wood shivers in antithesis of wrists
pinned to the last mile of mule brays,
a lissom frontface leaning to the left
edge of fledgling feathers flurrying
in a hint of happy accidents.

Molasses

shift
    sludge & sift
        impediments

    bending ooze
in sluice of
    sure sugars
    safe in tastes
        worn by other tongues

    the clump
    of what is not
        rum candy
    mats in the
    thrill of wheels
        blades & bevels

machines
      wish to squish
        said clod
        of god's food
          to mush
    tough slush

      too gooey

        to chew

Lair

If ripped jeans spring eternal
then journeys return to the tear
throwing intuition into crevice levity.

Leftover alibis allow the found
their finder's fee in the inner irk
of ears' perception.

Suggestive scents from the lair
will often lure honeybears
their plaintive entrapment.

Blip

Hyenas scamper in a badge
of blood—aardvarks angle
in a trudge of numbers
up the indigo hill

Terns see gulls as senior
believers in the sky's
dash for a splashing kill
in the flash of ample krill

Mine are the diamond days
of facet-fondling, rights
a-wronging in the flat soufflé
of a hero's buried habits

Noon peddles a copper cloud
mounted on a metal fetter
in the solar pantheon
of push-pull embryonics

Nights of the skyhawk
—sly nocturnal leggings
surpassed in flight
by a skippy rhythmic blip

Endgame

A crying violence
unbends the Wednesday
lemon
from its oval lodging,
green at the knobbly
tip a twist
of Tuesday's tangerine
hidden in
vacation eyelids

A sedentary lesion
festers in the depths
of grimace,
a gnash of choppers
rhythmic in their friction,
percussive
machinations
of adrenaline crush

Innuendo of a Lens

Sarcastic parkas in the sidewalk snow, a swollen elbow
of umbrellas. These movements reflect aquarium
dimension, suspended upended in an icicle cacophony.
A line of limp lamps, trashcans, strewn toys. A wall
of doubledoors, storefronts, barricaded corridors.
Allow foot leading knee…knees our human hinge…
calcium cartilage musclejoint monitors, everyday flexors.
Huddling here is tunnelvision precision, kinetic discourse,
a clutch of dubious roughtrade. A treble march,
the brazen task of buying up the future.
Steplightly nightly endeavor.

As circles in the sand so complement soaring seagulls,
a rhythmic ellipse the glimpse of God shiny shoreline
the moods of surf surface His world at one wink.
Observe the tinkling of water to rock, ocean junket,
muffled gull. A missed meal, yet the feel of absolute
fingers. Hide 'n' seek hideously tedious. The push
of paperclip and styrofoam cup to the lip of the desk.
Pencils reverberate with stale aspirations. Incriminations
emit from each ruined tip. Quelled breath spells
another lost ace in the payday parade.

Hotflash sacrificial DoveBar. A summer of harbor bellbuoys.
Hammock handiwork. A cord strung here, a hook hung there.
Imperial. Interior nets define spider practices. A little
latticework. Certain stitches embrace the buttock fabric,
what? Which fever of necessity this time? Which bubble
of intensity? Whose noose excuse? Spectral elegy, whose
beast of prey? Whose slave at the moment of harness,
whose tame getaway? This brace may stop you from:
laughing, talking, moving, working, skipping, thinking.

Rope of Mercy

I cling to the broken wing of belief
A dream singed at the soaring
A comet adrift in clipped cumulus intervention
resenting the cloudy curse of blocked suggestion

Yet bruised I chew words raw
A sonnet of sad anthems reverberates the vow
An ancient stale hello
throws cold winter to the skates

You're here in memory's glare
As fear-and-now
unfolds in the duality
of half-dreaming

Rearranging *what-ifs*
of stiff denial and claustrophobia
Blue in the face with begging
I bring a Rope of Mercy to the circle

Manchild

Impression travels far into the pits of reminiscence
Minutes stack alone by the key-type, keeping pace.
A shrill monktone climbs the gills
a lilting comedy of foot-in-the-mouth.
Flies squeak a hooray in the infant's tongue
Vowel openings escort the afterimage to a bar
with a single blinking light
Chunk tunas seeking the hook, all aboard.

Confession loves a quiet deepened by a book
It nips at the shirt of high unison
Unscrew the arm, sent by angels
Here on the cold floor
and leave it at that.
Over. Done.
Dawn costs us the bonny vowels.

Depression doesn't call, it stays.
Just when a lantern throws less light
Why a crow loves a crow
Squalled in timid hunger, spanked with love
Virus long in creeping, but underneath
Damages utter "fry me"
I am a thing to wear, a fat
Deep inside of worship, an old friend in town
Manchild, the fruits of my labor.

Smelts

Without rivets, smelts speak
of clawed cavities, limitless guises.

Gristmills of flavor
gone sparrow.

Tungsten Tone of a Silver Sky

I gobble eclectic ethnic and raw the common gamut
of fishhead flounders found round the corner of
Cannon & Spark. Peer in through the window a similar
plight, white rice and high prices, an impetuous bestiary
brazen with breathlessness. Soldiers step proud
in a loud and quizzical paltry pirouette of what's left
of the pensive afternoon.

Cheddar is the tip-of-the-tongue lipstick, critical
to the pose of rose-colored blackjack double-down
clowns on a summer's swing through the itchy ass
of Atlantic City. Take bets on the less-heeled
in the labor of exorbitant tough love in the closet
of inhibited logic. The uneasy hiss of Midas-touch
mothballs with their kiss-the-earth calling cards.

Late-night listeners tilt their jaws to raucously elevate
the noon to view nuclear nuggets all singed with
a central origin. Soon dawn rounds the tungsten tone
of a silver sky ripped by a dripping of descriptions
dry and thinly veiled predictions capsized rhapsodies
in a particularly playful peek into Doctor's fear
of the final breath.

Her Pink Twinkle

for Cindy Hochman

In a lapse of oscillation
a lad accepts a relic
a prelude to life-leaping
laundry a quandary of cozy
knishes in the meniscus
of meandering musk.

A baby periwinkle gloom
permeates the android arch,
a charged martyr a treadmill
of willing lepers, like *who slept here*
kind of lime-ice libation.
A gift for parched lips, miss.

A nubile monkey spectacle
wasted of necro-potency
embillicals in the wounded lisp
of a frigid prince in fragile times.
The forging of porcelain ornaments
disallows the shallow scepter.

Her pink twinkle preens a pose
on the rose agenda, basing her pattern test
on the Finocchio Series.
Heavensent bleary postcards sport pizzazz,
ring the White House lawn
within the skimming wind of a finch.

A Sooty Surfacing

If I were why a drip-dry tip, to tap or touch
when much is meant by the bordering.
Two bowls of curry a clear and ripe approach
too rosy as a dreamy leaf, tone-portal to possess.

A kind of typical tabby beneficence or worse,
the finite clinging. Casual walking stick, crook
akimbo minus bonus whiskerings, *tisk-a-task* to mask
or romp a pomposity of finicky permissions.

These growths astound the Mutant Wheeler
dealing for his cupcake mudpie in porridge squirts,
the mere intention a founder's fleeting nightmare.
The going grime a sooty surfacing, a mocking.

No quicker than a speeding ticket, no slower
than a pan-fried potato, this latent buddy-buddy
wormy yet awakened dusty flyleaf. That handsome
waistcoat of heavy scribblings in the kindest killing.

To Wit

Incidental as a slipped disc, a tweaked
knee, a clenched welt, seldom felt 'cept
where sheets erupt in a mean streak.
Bruises raise their scars in wars when
appearing nightly in the many mirrors
others flash whose wounds reflect
the warped slings and withered halters
hung from trophies' tarnished altars.

Grease engenders a gnashed attitude
imbued with high-octane anti-friction
restrictions.

Nipped in the Fibula

for John Cage

Soaring above the *Roaratorio*
of stone and sound are
Sumarian sisters Sumac warriors,
the taller with a trail
of drool along the lip of prank
and mystic urge. A lotus a clover
a roving spider rims off the ledge
of sedentary enemies
their furtive lunge a fearful fungus.

Nipped in the fibula are phantom acts
of random flow ripped from
the local stages of our chilly
new dark ages. A rage of wonder
unfurls in your intimate haste.
Embers of yesterday's lumber
pump ash into remnants of slumber
to remember the simple and
the sweet. A half a beat too late.

Rivals to my survival post
a low blow to my sternum along
the learning curve of hurt. Bursting in
was that first-rate slant of snow
a curious flurry of vegetable powder
a loose garlic salting of invisible pores
till they whelm in the veins
for a whirl of surface noise
and a candycane pearlescence.

Cucumber Slumber

Giddy of a gaunt preponderance. Agate. Earmark.
When weapons adhere to an ethereal theory. Abutment.
Atonement. The rose in you will swoon to the gardener's
tune. No framework can hold the glitter of gold. The
thinned threat of the penultimate. Ah, the Nikon icon. Apt
in the action a sly subtraction. Sell green dealers a grunt
and a grimace of pumice. Hummus among us in a soft
taco falafel. Neighbors' appraisal, a daisy-in-waiting.
Grace is that ace in the hole.

If culled from a rule of thumb. The rumination of a parsed
retort. A scuttle-boy. A skittered jigger. Knaves in the silo
a creationist supposition. Nouns put forth. A jelled
cohesion. New in this hemisphere a blinding blue concoction.
Trees of a leafy loss, grainy and of a tantalization.
Night pictures a Grecian meaning of a thing rethought.
The what's-in-it-for-me deliberation in the calm
of a cucumber slumber.

Sleepyhead Mumbles

Low borders of plumage resent
the fence in which they're penned,
a relentless maybe-mo
in the grid of no-go.

Sleepyhead mumbles accumulate
in the tweak of a nephew's knee.
A skee-ball in a penny arcade,
a late-life strife-ender
—like suspenders.

A sleuth of delusional refusals
institutional perusals
a glyph of a gutteral glitch
in the rich hurrah.

Suggest an etching
one slope in an otherwise
plainview portent, melodious
elves in appellate court.
A thwarted thumb
in the patented splint of entropy.

The Shatter

The shatter restructures, refragments agnostics,
impassions resentments of codefendants
in the mighty right of oral archery.

It splatters in silhouette
the levied debt of coiled
reparations.

We preach a perfect mother
in father's smother
of the other self.

A belief is wrenched from the bower.
The tower tolls power-hungry
or love-stung.

The bug is an endless tug at the whichway
we play partners in fluorescent
expectations.

Mulch

There's a fear called
rear-view mulch
which barricades the stay-at-home
    layers
distancing the glint of vapors
versed intuitively
          in mist

A systematical *rat-a-tat-tat*
throws reason
    to the Sioux

The ancient shank of sheep
sacrificed at the sad husk
of Famine's feebling
    enacts the whack of head
    and drain of lifeblood dribbling

    Of fear
    the near-sighted lamps
    stand darkly
        Badly amber blinds the stare
        dismissing flare of future-shock
            as night retards
            the guarded

    To open
    once the pinhole welcomes
    takes a seldom utilized allure
        to purify
        the present

Where the tension evanesces
in the pinch of weather's promise

    Titian sketches savoir-faire
        the lion's lair
        the heathen's hut

            Am I the why and how
                of ego's lessons?

Dervish Whirling

These sweeping gestures
lift pressure from my
prelim timidity
My minced hissy whisper
pauses
at the raw suicidal
lily
beside the floating
fern

These swifter currents
flurry
a harried waylaying
of cynic gloom
Fate steps in
and waters the faucets
of eyelids
long dry
from inattention

I'm mourning
my ol' used-to-be
still debt penetrates
my artful heart

Yes you've chiseled chinamen,
christened ships
from other ports,
And here
you're inching toward
a duality of islands
Raisins of praise
and rich
sifting sandstorms

I'm somehow warmer
now your
handfuls of hope
sent a-sky
have cut a healthy gash
through my chestals

I can laugh
without a raincloud
I can linger
and bravely put my finger
to the lip of loss

I write this
willow-whisper
wandering the keys,
wishing more than
quarters in the slot

These seconds
float closer
Scarred heart
alert this wakened brain
Hey babe I'm late
for teenage tantrums

You ruffled
my sluggish
clumsy clamoring caution
and spilling out
were fountains
of free-range drifting dreams
Sifting silt
in the billowing

3

Highwire Acts

Holy Hiss   *for Hart Crane*

A holy hiss bestows its kiss
in the bristle of twigs
or breeze bending branches
the wind whining low

The breath of thieves whistling in the lurk
gives substance to such emotion
as to answer singing crickets
their quizzical mysteries

Ewes lick a wounded wan battalion
Bees blend intent upon their favored flower
and monotonous lies swarm morbidly
A swish of whispers and a cough

Wait — dare we forget the threat of doors
closing — *click* — stark in their locks,
The boxer's fingers in a sweaty sponge
gloved in the oven of his mission?

Climates aerially approve the meandering
melancholy of gray continental cloudswells
Swiftly a towel enwraps a dripping dad
his Timex ticking still

Invariably in transit we persist
to spray our personal pollen
and thrust a tethered nerve
through shivered leaves of stress

Day's azure holds its zones in motion
only to finally flicker pink and falter
Sending Morpheus to issue ethereally
his very thimble of tiny stars

Distanced by a Wish

Ten's my limit
of a thinned beneficence
buoyed of a belfry

A "deem" mendicant
snugs a glyph of "pixel"
sentenced to the stew of usual

A voice thick in asthma sockets
coughs a collective heave
in the eddy-breath of running waters

Timids attract tomatoes,
their ridges torn by younger thumbs
A wield of skimmed immensities
distanced by a wish

february's ferocious affirmation

february's ferocious affirmation
dim and windows barren
bitter winter snowdrift rainy
before the patented plow

nor frigid the wiggle room
unpredictable I-you showdown
slowed to creepy feet
and glistening dust-off

so new the usual wants
in heydays haunting
I reach back to blacken
any remaining gremlins

a study of inverted pleasures
mentoring the measurements
a chew of a candy kiss
the shatter of observant matter

Maelstrom

Would you like to see your face in a favorite maelstrom,
daft in the reassurance that no candidate ever stooped
to the fallacies of false feeling?

Would there be a pundit pandering to percentages,
positioned in the erratic goof of a sly infarction,
damned to be lassoed into innuendo?

Do you see wool as dividing lamb and cattle,
glueing rude Sunday to Wednesday-*yawn* Thursday
in gainful unemployment of an intellectual?

Do they wave wands over our baskets,
when we can't even lend a five to the widow
who sorts morticians from beauticians?

When it hesitates, does it vegetate,
the gelatin seconds to the fore,
your work in a drawer?

Do they mellow, the low equations, comedians
of youth, the nervous curtseys, the courteous
vultures guzzling true rent of the mansion in flame?

Does it hear you, the humming,
when a footfall dodges cemeteries,
sly in velocity, the audacity of a tumor?

Does she rumor your approval, the nude in future-glass,
shattered by philosophies costing pretty penny
in a scheme of noose and vanity?

Do they poke the wicked, or pretend to
when the little presents all unravel
at your door when no one's listening?

Do the gardeners all take turns in mowing
the cold facts of engineering
with a cross lowered in fooling?

Is "cautious" liquescent to the eccentric,
or does "bandage" breathe a loose eclipse,
where "fortuitous" knew no booty?

Is the garbage all charred and gnarled
in society's earring, all yipping
for quarters and nickels cylindrically?

Is his paunch all pampered, the yearner
querying vicissitudes of earnest,
curling at the boot of his mistress?

Do they give up the cup,
or take up the lip
when a weapon's been dropped?

Inimitable

Inimitable bubble bursting bad news Susan sifting
pygmies, September Song along for the rich aroma.
I'm ninety-five. A nuisance, a nemesis, a fathomable
foment. Incensed a denser sorrel.

Lift buttocks and bleat a ready dread. Candidly
a kosher closure.

Fervid trunk-like lids, decisions smile of lye and limits.
Distanced rondelet, a look-see, a peeping wallet.
He's wheezing raisins, sorting forks and knife-shafts.
I laugh a purple lull, that fabled pill.

She rings her arms in wet cement, dame of sewn
seasons, mowed lawns, dead leaves, known secrets.
She turns fact into fable, glass into tables, cash
into coin. I'm known for the sale of wily wills.

Pyrex Bowl

I'd eagle-eye a Pyrex bowl lowering my beak
to the tooth of despair. A bleary morn-tossed
lost night's sleepy pincers lay peach upon
my melon ball in a call-out for happy campers.

I drive a peony corridor crazy with roseates
of still night and bidden kindnesses, distressed
only glowing, one inner ear extant in a gaunt
hurdy-gurdy of worry beads aimed at headwaiters.

Gone is the wrong side of taproot maps and
stripped are donnybrooks of the usual look-see
in your penitence pertaining to amazement.
So aroused yet so absent, bent and banished.

We who tickle too easy, berserk after Balzac,
attracted to the spaces between. It's the hum
of crushed watch dials in buzzing barns…. I'd warn
the Florentine of facts too fuzzy to figure.

Eager Fingers

Surely I'll allow a cowbell to dart hither
& thither and sound its saccharine tones
if a rooster should *commonplace*
a repeatable crowing.
These chapters capture the afterburn
of a nervous Nell, her veggie lifespan
at most a tattered, taunting hoax.

When U.S. senators spank the monkey,
we surmise a cattail of lovely labels,
a tabletop of neat & tidy napkins
to ease the grease of eager fingers.
A Sunday snapshot propped
by a steady hand
inverts the vanishing vista.

No sign of avarice slugging a greedy credo.
It's the nearsighted needy who speak
to my inner goggles, a shaft
of giggles reining me in.
See, I'm slim as I am plump—
in another light a dialed-in princess,
her fond access to the throne.

Degrees of daggers decompress upon
the western whirl in a swirling minute.
A coterie of cooing doves does double duty,
clawing free from cavities of courageous
canvas drippings and dropcloth dribbets.
We swivel clean of maternal mumblings
upon the blank equator.

Lady Wah leaves me raw to the sulky
Slavic syndrome, voluptuous violins
vamping to the tramp inside.
Sore as an orchestra out of cheat sheets,
we cling to the meager template
of talking to ourselves
on the shelf of *show me the way*.

Tympani

I concur with a simmer
stirring the tympani
tapping out a bassy cadence
boosting acoustically
my wrangled anguish

Grist Wistful

Of grist its wistful thrift
Of grim its limb-to-limb
Boon trellis. *Fait d'or.* Morphine
torpid on the tongue.

Twin friend famine flurry. Turret arc.
Turbine engine. Finesse a stress
of sorrow. Gnarled.

Light blessing over bones. Frozen
arctic, trip in transit. Dense
or western wind.

Seems wheat stands on its own
Sown seed, autumn harvest
Dusk offers germing husk, ex-chaff.

A Palm's Proximity

Flicker of friendship drips
a shy dagger of a decision
residing in the lingo
of lost lovers on a bender

Zircon rings let us modulate
a rural flock of affirmations
Azure tassels of a thread
too fine to refigure

Because a syringe of sadness
hampers the clock's reminders,
we swoon before a flood
of furry remnants of betrayal

Are you ending the tinkle
of wink-elements talkative?
We've waited or debated
or hibernated what's ours

Dissolve an olive, dethrone
the roan pony of his hearse
nursing a hassle-free
promise of a palm's proximity

Mother rakes an ingrate
offspring over the putty
of petty impositions
for opposing the family way

Now in the near-nuisance
of mercenary armament
the plucky argument is cuff-proud
and sweater-ready

Is there a terrible time limit
to our trying, or is this
one edge of it — my
tiny aortic toy in transit?

Everywhere a spare part
of infinite recombination
recoiling at the momentary
amplification of echo-loss

Are we a tweaked tongue
among the mood-incumbents
who'd scurry in the worry-flow
of would-be contenders?

Lucent

When whales salivate
I'll shake a brainstorm
free of keepsake variety
in the huddle of a poodle

Lucent words their urge
solidified in fragrant ladies
summering in a wayward
yearning for peripherals

Songs to Your Pores

Tom's pistol-packin' mama
a stern observer a reverb unique
to weakening the preacher's knees,
a cuppa hot Postum a sleek
Panasonic audio board if untoward
the lotion I don to sing pearly
songs to your pores.

Witness this guess a lesson looped
a pet left at the altar of luck
unlearning the pluperfect
tense as a jury in waiting.

Wrigglish the tweak
of the terminally ticked off,
the raw sewage of sagely advice.
A rice patty melt a svelte
and shiny set of shoes
at a harlequin bargain.

Motto

Moods contain rainforests and sporadic winds
equivalent to silly feelings, bare necessities
or aggravations, sounding out plantercorn particles
participating in platitudes, studious in flattery
steamed once lightly under glass, at last
impassioned, defueled ascender, spent of life's
infinite futures.

If None Be the Number

for Gerard Manley Hopkins

If flimsy whims spew skewed flaws
slightly ajar with raw fire, then wring
my free reeling will its wheeling worth,
a tenth of might my meteor.

If few be elegant my names
for your sculpted face
ascending the ranks of speakless reach,
then wrest the empty nuggets out
from my dryest mouth.

If none be the number of my shy praises
for your lady's ways
your wordy whims your pudding hands
your fairest yes
then damn be the curse that lay upon
the pale brown earth
one bleary skyless desert-riddled dearth

If woe be the silence I pay
with awkward artifice,
the lisp that lingers in long reminders
then I, witness of your favored features,
must pay endless cash unkind
ever-mourned by my sad hand laden
with hardened time.

Shazzam

She's shades of slurry
firmly flowing needwards
A sieve of leave-me-not
proclamations

I'm a blue streak fleeced
by immense propensity
Faux-friendly
loving every vindictive river

I'll stand between
dry dock and the nighthawk
A dim mind's eye
roaming moments

Immovable mule

Shazzam inflammable

Scrawl

These fields in fallen times a winding road of cloak-
and-dagger candidates. I watch a startled gray attainment
of name-loss on the causeway. No sweat is a better place.
Pure ransom a boozy lunacy. No pricks spawned a prayer
of ne'er-do-wells. A mock talkative, a moot melange.
Wiser is a trace of patterned knives, a set of seesaw
thrashers, resplendence in a broody penance.

Jumpstart a hilly milieu the hull of habitation. Dotweiler's
antics a stroll down mammary lane. Behold the train
a-comin' red rum and tundra funneling a lukewarm drizzle.
Distanced in the wisteria a periwinkle purpose. Nervous Nell
in appellate courtship to skinny-dip in old Pinter's pond.
The long and short of itsy-bitsy teeny-weeny track marks.
The scrawl of wild piracy.

Consorting with the alias a stray sharpshooter's worn-out
weapons. To manage more in five minutes than a Turk
in workday woolens. Risen of a Hindenburg system save
a sirloin steak, the walkway papers presume no pursuit as we
summer in Spain. Do you hear the pitter-patter of puddles
accenting the scant shadowy gnarling of *feed the kitty?*
A city skillet of intestinal wheretofores.

> Innate the freight of armed farmers.
> Disintegrate the wait-and-see.

Skids

From these skids darts the resolution
to be famous within four walls.

Say sloth, and this gas is
his favored flask. Studied rub.

And if these dreams seem meant for cement,
then twenty would be greener a resourcefulness.

Gravy. It quiets. They stay.

Does it double in the curving?
Do they hover in the oven? Over, verily.

Broken in. Ill at ease.
Trial and terror.

Club rub. If in agreeing, a long hollow.
And of course, a regular.

Nights of Giverny

Light as a bite of balsa wood
the tea-garden martyr
dissipates in the late-night
white-hot glare of Golgotha.

Ah the nights of Giverny
and yes Montpelier
the racy eyes of encounter.
A roundabout pout-and-mope pirouette,
a slick and neighborly way
of skipping the bare essentials.

Decide nice in the navel of adversarial
The burial of accumulated myrrh
in the clergy
of ecclesiastic enthusiasm
Less one avid merchant
in the lethal diamond dream.

Raunchy

Let these skinny
lines plead my
ailing case

I'm slain
by the bounty
of your bosom

Look I'm drunken
sloppy high
a silly shambles
of myself

I've been wrecked
I'm raunchy
honey utterly
intoxicated
by your beckoning
echo

O let my spasm
warm your chasm

Midnight Spikes

Midnight spikes pry a reticular cunning,
spun gold with lipstick moorings.
I ziplock a tick-tock wristwatch
only to glad-wrap my half-baked sandwich.

If doubts malinger (and they do)
then this wretch curdles a light diet
of bird droppings swept clean
by a brittle windy whooosh.

I shiver to think all is shadrack and shady maidens
living in a cave. It's all too *run-of-the-malady
roll-of-the-dice.* I come to you soured and briny
a dill citizen about to revive his dying dream.

Banister *for Lewis Warsh*

Twin hymn humming roomy views a Tuesday
noose and straddle pocked of a thicket
prized in a seesaw of raw rhetoric.

She's eaten a dreamer glad of hand
and heart of ice a trimester combo
of woofing unmentionables.

Don't overextend plenitude a driving seacrest
lathed of blueprints bathed in splashes
of white light upon the banister.

Gloveless of a stubborn motion mounted
with an upturned hand I stay erased
to the theater of selections.

Time explodes the frozen in a thinly-veiled
thawing, conscious of a recalled hubcap
daft in the pool of currents.

Nowhere is there goof-proof paint which
props its ready drips in a perception pan
...the princess and the pea.

I was mistaken in the idea that they could
track me with their digital data-lenses
browsing my shadow habits.

Numbed but a buttercup puptent the crash
of a tapestry ripped in a purple lump
of keenly felt fluidity.

While earthquake prediction is an inexact
science, tremors form a nemesis
to swift lodgings in the hills.

Dry Zion upswale the horde of miners
and fortune-seekers, a tough denim hinged
upon a bruised and buckling knee.

Reality Knishes for Ginsberg

In Memoriam April 1997

The beard was ever Allen
bound to steer the moral mirror
your direction

Alternative
religion ultraconscious search
for something like an art of living

Gatekeeper chronologist prophet preacher
Task of raising rabbinical conscience
Flexing societal muscles
                              the mind

Icon poet who slips thru the comb
of mass neglect concerning
Artists as a race

Even punks today have turned an ear
to where you stood in flames
in Beat's eternal blues

Ginzi
Your curly knobbly lectures
licked the lip of listeners
You made critics even howl
Leper-sexed and hungry
Seeking great spirit of the universe
in terrible godly form
Allen Ginsberg says this: I am
a mass of sores & worms
& baldness & belly & smell

The poet-laureate of the Beat Generation
wrote a dozen short poems just last
Wednesday at his home in the East Village
before he slipped into a coma

Paper words! Fblup! Fizzle! Droop!

First thought   best thought
Better catch it 'fore it flees
Instants   ideas
Green leaves on autumn trees
seem forever
Yet the mind that thrills at birthing
must fix on paper   or on tape
or on disc   or online
the art of traveled dreamscape

You place your hand before your beard
with awe
You invent ways of tracing windows
of translating reality to the page
without the frills of centuries ago
A moral Pound a modern Whitman
Ecstatic to yourself the flesh
The fuel of truths

Allen howled so all who hear no evil
see no evil   speak no evil
would at least rethink their meek aversion
to the laws of inner voice

Bequest

I bequeath breath
a braying death

A laughing in the face
of glaciers

Apostrophizing
a pale unknown

The subtle strafing
of negation

Mitch Corber is a New York City poet who has been writing and performing his work since the early 1980's. A NY Foundation for the Arts fellow, he is director-videographer of cable TV's long-running weekly series Poetry Thin Air and the founder of the educational poetry DVD archives, thinairvideo.com. Studying poets he's documented has contributed to his evolving style as a writer. Mitch is a founding member of the innovative multimedia art collective, Colab (Collaborative Projects).

photo Minnie Berman